Exploring nature with Georges en Daiko

10 Birds in our backyard.

"A bird doesn't sing because it has an answer, it sings because it has a song."

Maya Angelou

Link to youtube where you can explore together Birds in our backyard: https://youtu.be/U6VCuChjbcg

GeorgesDaiko.com

Reading is everything. Discover new worlds. Learn to read together exploring nature.

Link to GeorgesDaiko.com

D/2024/15889/18

This book belongs to

....

Good morning, great tit. You sing cheerfully and loudly. You are also always well dressed with your black tie!
Thanks, Daiko. Would you like to sing along? Ti-ti-tu!

GREAT TIT

Small colorful bird
Length? 14 cm – 5.5 inches
Weight? 17 g – 0.6 ounces

Where? Everywhere there are trees. Gardens, forests, and cities.

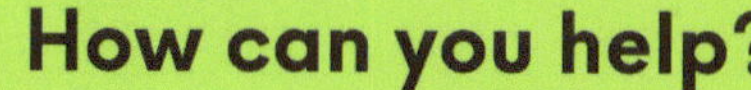

How can you help?
Nest box
Bird feeder with fat balls and sunflower seeds

Black head with white cheeks

Yellow breast with black stripe

The great tit is known for its wide range of songs

Food?
Insects
Spiders
Seeds & nuts

Hello blue tit. You look like the great tit. But dressed as Zorro.
I'm a little smaller, a little sweeter, and I have more colors! Who is Zorro?

BLUE TIT

Small bird
- Length? 12 cm – 4.7 inches
- Weight? 10 g – 0.35 ounces

Where? Gardens, parks, forests.

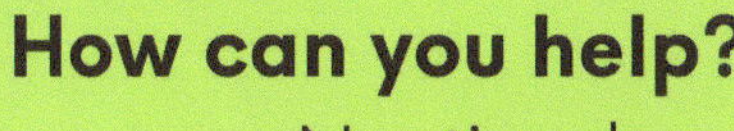

How can you help?
Nesting box
Bird feeding table
with fat balls and
sunflower seeds

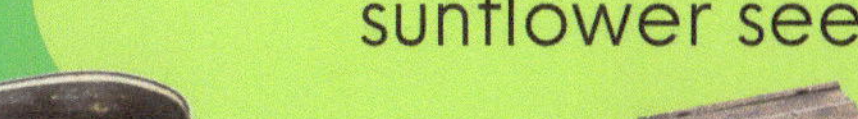

Yellow breast
with blue wings

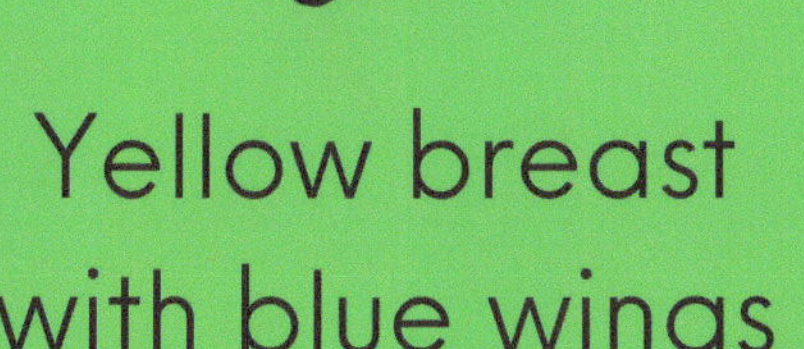

Blue hat
White head
Line through eye

Food?
- Insects
- Spiders
- Seeds, nuts

ZORRO?

Zorro (= Spanish for fox) was a hero with a black mask who fought bad guys to help the poor and innocent people. He used a sword to leave a "Z" as a sign that he had been there.

Who would win? Zorro or the Blue Tit?

Hi house sparrows. There are so many of you!
We like to live together in a large group. Chirp Chirp.

HOUSE SPARROW

Little brown bird
- Length? 14 cm – 5.5 inches
- Weight? 17 g – 0.6 ounces

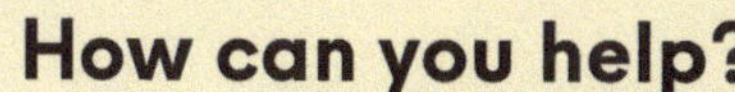

How can you help?
Nesting boxes
apartment
Bird feeding table
with kernels and crumbs

Where? Around the house, in towns and villages.

Gray crown

Striped
back

Thick beak
Black chin
White cheek
patch

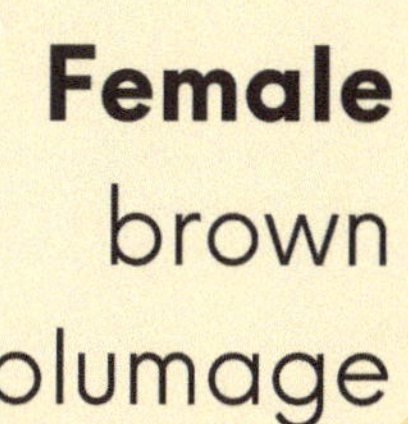

Female
brown
plumage

Food?
- Insects
- Cereals
- Seeds
- Crumbs

Daag huntjes, wei es et met uuch?
What is Mr. Finch saying?
He speaks a dialect from Belgium. He's asking how we are doing.

CHAFFINCH

Colorful bird
- Length? 15 cm - 6 inches
- Weight? 25 g - 0.9 ounces

Where? Wherever there are trees. Forests, parks, gardens and cities.

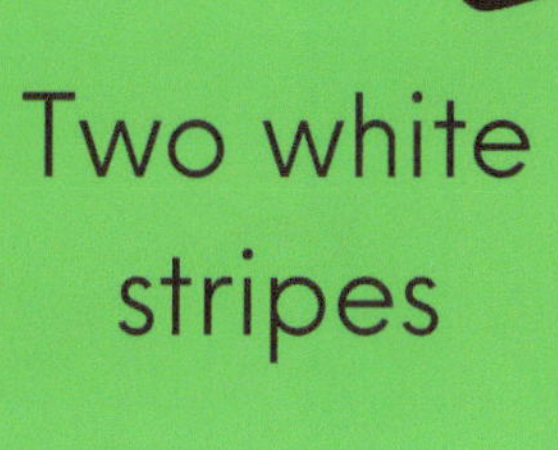

Two white stripes

Grey-blue crown

Broad beak

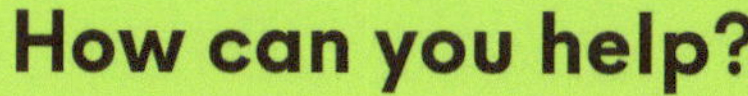

Food?
- Insects
- Seeds
- Beechnuts

Well, well, if it isn't the feathered messengers of the sky! Greetings, pigeons!
Coo-coo Coo-coo

WOOD PIGEON

Larger bird that likes company.
- Length? 41 cm – 16 inches
- Weight? 500 g – 18 ounces

Where? City squares, parks and gardens.

How can you help?

Feeding spot
Nesting location

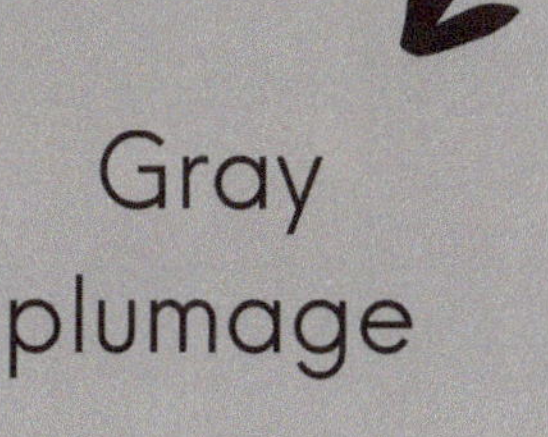

Gray
plumage

Green and white
spot on neck

Pink colored
chest

Food?
- Crops (grain)
- Seeds
- Worms

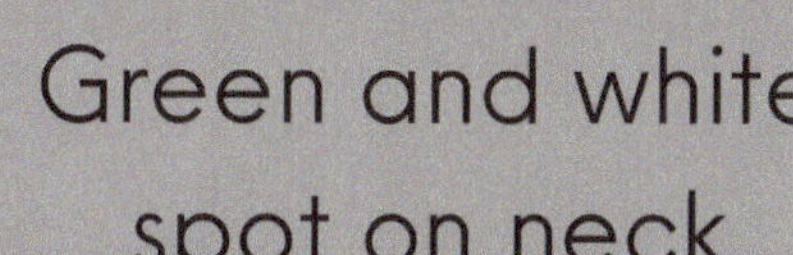

Hello Mr and Mrs Blackbird! Where are your friends?
We prefer to live alone or with the two of us.

BLACKBIRD

Dark bird
- length? 25 cm - 10 inches
- weight? 100 g - 3.5 ounces

Where? Gardens, forests, parks, shrubbery, cities.

How can you help?

Place shrubs and trees for nests and food

Orange-yellow beak and eye rim

Completely black (female brown)

Food?
- Worms
- Snails
- Fruits

hello starling.
hello starling.
How are you starling?
How are you starling?
Why are you repeating after me?
Why are you repeating after me?

STARLING

A flock of birds
- Length? 20 cm – 8 inches
- Weight? 80 g – 3 ounces

Where? Cities, parks and reed stems.

How can you help?

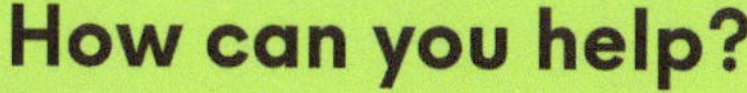

Nesting box
Rotting fruit
to the ground

Shiny green-
black plumage

Long, pointed
yellow beak

Food?
- Insects
- Fruit

STARLING

Murmuration
Starling cloud

This is my garden!
Not true! I was here first.
Actually this is my garden. But you are both welcome!

ROBIN

Small territorial bird
- Length? 14 cm – 5.5 inches
- Weight? 17 g – 0.6 ounces

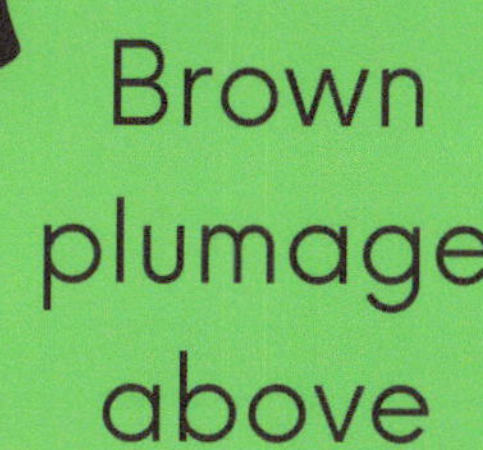

How can you help?
Birdhouse
Feeding spot

Where? Gardens, forests and parks.

Narrow beak

Red chest and face

Brown plumage above

Food?
- Insects (Narrow beak)
- Worms
- Spiders
- Berries and fruits

Hello wren!
Hello Georges, where is Daiko? Are you cold? What is your favorite color? What do you like to eat?

WREN

Very small curious bird
- Length? 10 cm – 4 inches
- Weight? 7 g – 0.25 ounces

Where? Gardens and dense shrubbery.

Short tail up

Brown plumage

Narrow beak

Hello Chiffchaff! There you are. I've been looking all over for you.
Chirp, chirp. I was on holiday in Spain. The food by the sea was yummy. Chirp, chirp.
Hooray, spring is coming!

CHIFFCHAFF

Little nervous bird
- Length? 12 cm - 5 inches
- Weight? 7 g - 0.25 ounces

Where? Forests and gardens.

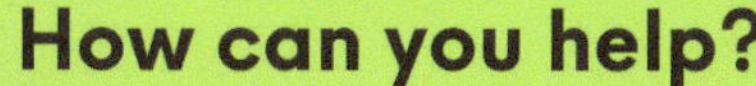

How can you help?

Birdhouse

Brown-green
plumage

Light stripe
above the eye

Yellowish breast

Delicate beak

Eten?
- Insects

POSTCAR
Introducing...
for Spring...
The Chiffchaff's song, a happy tune, tells us that spring will be here soon!

BIRDS

Which birds do Georges and Daiko meet?

Which birds do Georges and Daiko meet?

My Birdwatching Checklist

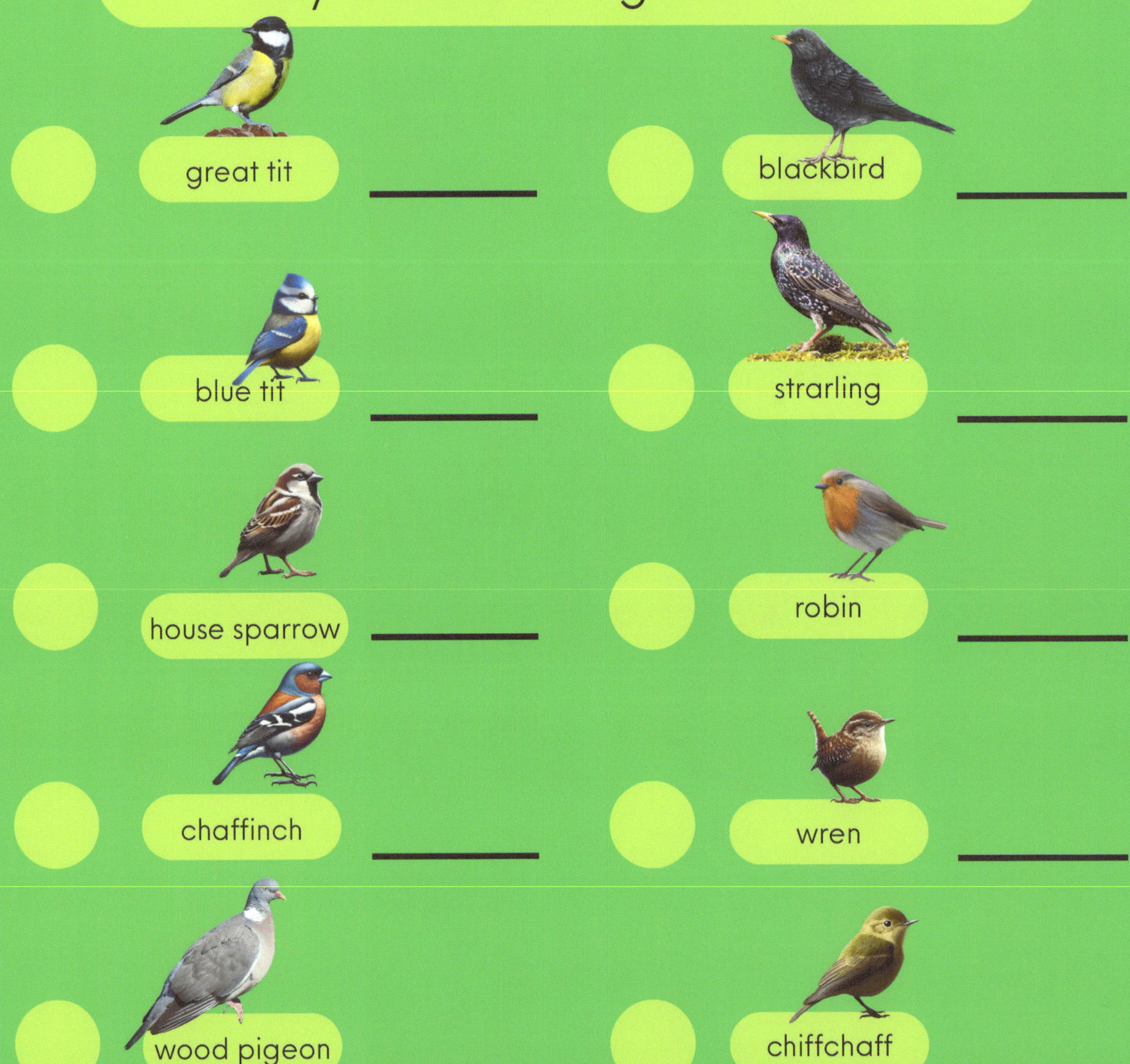

Birdwatching Bucket List

rock pigeon

mallard duck

common loon

northern cardinal

great blue heron

black-capped chickadee

blue jay

barn owl

yellow warbler

bald eagle

Ruby-throated Hummingbird

common kingfisher

toucan

bearded vulture

peregrine falcon

My favorite bird:

Picture or drawing:

Tips for Birdwatching

- Bring binoculars and a field guide.
- Wear neutral-colored clothing.
- Be quiet and move slowly.
- Note the size, shape, color, and behavior of the birds.
- Visit different habitats to see a variety of species.
- Watch and listen! Use the Merlin app!

Interesting app:
Merlin. Helps you recognize the sounds of birds in your garden!

Links:
* https://www.vogelgeluid.nl/
* https://www.natuurpunt.be/

Exploring nature with Georges en Daiko

Reading list	date	Rating

Adventures

1 – Where is the ball?
2 – Party time!
3 – The rainbow.
4 – Big stick, small stick.
5 – The zoo.
6 – The dino egg.

Exploring nature

1 – 10 birds in my backyard.
2 – 10 birds of prey.
3 – 10 feathered friends.
4 – 10 trees.

My books: